MOTHER'S   MUSINGS

The Poetry and Songs
Of Judy Tinsman

Julia Belle (Walker) Tinsman

"The Poetry and Songs of Julia Belle (Walker) Tinsman"
Also known as Judy Tinsman
Poetry and Songs written between
1930 and 1998
Copyright © 2014 by Julia B. Tinsman
Look Up Publishing Company

ISBN-13: 978-0692305164

Transcribed from original
and hand-written pages,
with minimal copy editing,
by the poet's daughter-in-law,
Angela Tinsman

If a talent is given,
By God to you
To put tho'ts into rhyme,
Use it my friend
To lift fellow men
And help them redeem the time.

For, A poem is more than just A rhyme
It's the beat of A heart,
The turn of A mind.
It can portray Christ,
Lived in your time
Yes, A poem is more than just A rhyme.

Julia (Judy) Tinsman

Mother's   Musings

POETRY

A Poem is More than Just a Rhyme

A poem is more than just a rhyme.
It's the beat of A heart,
The turn of a mind.
It portrays A life
Lived in its time
Yes, A poem is more that just A rhyme.

It can shine A light,
In the darkness of night
Or dull the sharp edge of pain
It can bring beauty,
Where all was drab,
And life where death had lain.

Tho'ts can turn upward,
Which were so low,
By reading A bit of verse
Words can be softer,
And kind and good,
Which once had been A curse.

Hope can be brightened,
To shine anew,
Where discouragement had been
Faith can be born,
In A heart once cold,
By singing A song or hymn.

If A talent is given,
By God to you
To put tho'ts into rhyme
Use it my friend
To lift fellow men,
And help them redeem the time.

For, A poem is more than just A rhyme
It's the beat of A heart,
The turn of A mind.
It can portray Christ,
Lived in your time
A poem is more that just A rhyme.

My Poems
Julia B. Walker 1930

I am a childish poet
I am not big you see
And if my poems are not good
You can just excuse me.

I like to write about nature
And pretty things I see
Oh I love them all
Because Jesus gave them to me.

I love the trees and flowers
I wish they could understand what I say
There is one thing you must not do
Is throw your words away

You might as well just write them down
And save your words today
For you might run out of words
And then you would be sorry
You threw your words away.

You must go to the home of a sick one
And give the words to them
It might make them feel happy and bright
And make them well again.

So you must start saving
Your many words today
And don't never, never, never
Throw your words away.

Jesus Is Ever With Me

Julia B. Walker   1930

Jesus is ever with me
And with him I will stand
For someday He will meet me
Upon the golden strand.

And so I must help others
To get started on the way
For Jesus is coming to get me
And take me home someday.

I want others to be ready
When He comes floating down
And also like me
Receive a golden crown.

I know I shall be happy
And many others too
For those who worked for Jesus
Will then be angels too

And then we'll sing around Him
And praise His holy name
And we will still serve Jesus
          Our king forever to reign.

The Weakest Link
Revised, 1953

A chain is only just as strong
As its weakest link we know
So the tests and trials of life must come
That the weak might stronger grow.

We may boast and say we're sure
Our faith will take us through
But we're only as strong as we prove to be
In the tests that we go through

Tho' the night be long and winds are high
And billows leap and foam
Don't be dismayed, 'twill soon be day
God careth for His own.

I Am Sure That He Cares About Me

I am sure that He cares about me
There is nothing I can hear or can see
And wherever I may go
Jesus knows about it so
I am sure that He cares about me

I am glad that He cares about me
When He hung on the cruel cruel tree
When His blood was dripping red
I'm persuaded that it said
How great was the love He had for me

I am glad that I learned to love too
That I might have a greater love for you
That I might point the way
To a bright eternal day
And never be a stumbling block unto you

Yes, love is a universal tongue
It's understood by old and young
If a burden you can bear
And I help and I care
I am sure Jesus' praises will be sung

He said, "If ye love one another"
Let the world know that you're brothers
We won't get in his way
And he can truly say
            I know that my brother cares about me

This World God Has Made
Winter, 1958-1959

I love all nature God has made
    From the very tallest tree
To the tiniest little blade of grass
    Or moss that I can see

I love the rocks and mountains
    The valley and the plain
I love the warmth of sunshine
    The gentle fall of rain

I love the deep blue of the sky
    I love the stars at night
The harmless firefly too, you know
    As it shows its little light

I love the seasons of the year
    The spring and, yes, the fall
The summer and the winter, too
    For the great God made them all

Spring
Winter, 1958-1959

I feel the breezes blowing
    I see flowers here and there
And as the grass grows greener
    I know, spring is in the air

I feel the warmth of sunshine
    Heard birds calling to their mate
Gathering bits of straw or feather
    To build their nest before 'tis too late

The brook is thawed and bubbling
    As it moves on to the sea
The tiny leaves are bursting forth
    From every branch and tree

And I feel new life springing forth
    As I rise to duty, too
Of all the seasons that there is
    I love spring best, don't you?

Spring and Its Beauties

I love the springtime flowers
I love the grass so green.
I love to see the bubbling brook
As in the spring is seen.

Everything so beautiful
As pretty as can be
When everything comes back to life
I love it, can't you see

I love the many animals
They're flavoring to spring
I love them all and every one
Yes, I love everything

Do you wonder why I love them?
Whether great or small
The reason I will give you is
The Lord God made them all

The Beautiful Things of Spring
Julia B Walker

One day I saw a little bird
Sitting in a tree
Every time I looked at him
He'd nod and chirp at me

He was not such a tiny bird
But he was a pretty fellow
His breast was red his back was black
And his little bill was yellow

He'd chirp and sing in the beautiful spring
And in the winter weather
He'd fly away, yes, far away
To a land much warmer and better.

I love the many little birds
The flowers and everything
There is so many beautiful things
In this season we call spring

The brooklet is so peaceful
As it meanders along
Minding its own business
And singing a little song.

The trees are all budding
With leaves and pretty flowers
The limbs and branches of the trees
Are like heaving towers

The grass is green and beautiful
Waving in the breeze

It seems very small indeed
By the side of those towering trees.

I love them all and every one
They are so green and pretty
My heart in love goes out to them
And will throughout eternity

Ah! Spring is Here
Julia Walker

Hear the little brooklet
Ah! Spring is in the air
I see it, I feel it
Ah! It is every where.

It's in the murmuring brooklet
It's in the flowers gay
It's in the morning sunshine
Of this bright, spring day.

It's in the budding apple trees
The peach trees and the pear
It's even in the dewdrops
Ah! It is every where.

Even the little violets
Are a sign of spring
It makes me happy and I feel
That I love everything.

The sunshine, flowers and the birds
Tell us that spring is here
And I'm only sorry
That it comes just once a year.

Spring
Julia B. Walker   1930

How I love the sunshine
And how I love the spring
When once again you can hear
The birds so sweetly sing

And then there's flowers springing up
And blooming everywhere
There's lilac, violets and daisies
And dandelions here and there

There are many beautiful flowers
That comes along with spring
When the brooklet sees them
He begins to sing

Springtime
Julia B. Walker   1930

When the grass becomes so green
And the birds begin to sing
Then the children also sing
For once again they know tis spring

When the flowers blossom
When the children dance and sing
Then everyone is happy
For once again they know tis spring.

One Night
Judy Walker, 12 years old

One night 'twas dark and dreary
No stars were in the sky
It was hot and dry and choking
The breeze heaved a heavy sigh

The moon shone blood red
Against the darkened sky
Upon my haunted maison
That towered to the sky.

I went to bed at eleven o'clock
I was sleepy but could not sleep
I thought I heard murmuring voices
Away in the shadows deep

I looked out in the darkness
Just across the way
I saw the ghostly tombstone
For there the graveyard lay.

The Sunshine On a Cloudy Day
Julia B. Walker   1930

I love the pretty sunshine
Although on a cloudy day
It goes and hides behind the clouds
And won't come out to play

No matter how you beg him
No matter how you yell
He seems to stay up there and hide
But why! He will not tell.

He must be afraid of the thunderstorm
For he hides up there all day
It seems that he just sits and mourns
And wont come out to play.

The whole world seems more happier
With the sun than without
I just cannot understand why
And what it is about.

He must be just sad today
Or else he isn't well
But why he don't come out and play
Is something he won't tell.

Leaves Do Fall
Winter, 1958-1959

I saw the leaves turn red and gold,
   Fall softly to the ground
And I tho't how life is passing
   Without murmur or a sound.

Do we realize how short our life,
   Or, how quickly time goes by,
Do any of us living now
   Know just when we will die?

We often hear folks, careless say,
   "Oh, I've more time than money".
No preparation made for death
   Folks, these things aren't funny.

We know, as sure as autumn comes,
   The leaves are sure to fall
We know, too, as we grow old,
   Death surely comes to all.

Then why do we go careless on,
   Each day and month and year,
Knowing soon the time will come
   To leave our place down here?

Knowing, too, we're unprepared
   We've sinned against our neighbor.
We've sinned against our Father, too,
   In most our earthly labor.

So, dear ones, won't you go to God,
   And on Him loudly call?
Time is swiftly running out
   As sure as leaves do fall.

The Lovely Time of Year

Julia B. Walker, 1930

I love the pretty summertime
And the birds that sweetly sing
And the pretty flowers too.
That bloom early in the spring

I also love the spring time
When the grass first gets so green
Whereupon the fields and meadows
There the dandelions may be seen.

But best of all is the fall
When the leaves turn red and gold
But soon it will be winter
And the leaves will die and mold.

Thanksgiving

Julia B. Walker   1930

Thanksgiving time is here
With its joy and with its cheer
And now we must thank again
Our loving Master dear.

So let us celebrate this day
For our Savior dear
To thank Him for the things He's did
For us throughout the year.

We can't forget Thanksgiving Day
Which comes to us each year
For I know that we must thank Him
For His love and kindly cheer.

Snowflakes Falling

Julia B. Walker   1930

Oh! See the pretty snow flakes
That fall so fast and thick
The ground will soon be covered
    If they fall fast and thick

The snowflakes are so pretty
They are so pure and white
Just see how they flutter
    They fly with all their might

How I love to see the snowflakes
They cover grass and all
Everything seems so beautiful
    As the snowflakes fall.

Lesson of the Snowflakes
Winter, 1958-1959

I mused as watching snowflakes,
    Fall gently from the sky
As one upon another,
    Covered field and meadow nigh.

One snowflake cannot cover much
    Nor melted make much water
So we cannot do much alone
    Unless helped by our Father

If we but have a purpose
    That's noble fine and true
If we'll but work together
    As snowflakes always do

Then much could be accomplished
    While we travel here below
If we'd just all work together
    As the falling of the snow.

The Babe In The Manger

Julia B. Walker   1930

I can't forget when in Bethlehem
Of the baby who in a manger lay
So the babe so dear and holy
Is our Savior in heaven today

He guards us and helps us;
And keeps us each day
He guards and helps
    In every way
So that child who in the manger lay
Is our Savior in heaven today

Christmas Joy
Julia B. Walker, 1930

Christmas time is coming
Little children humming
And the Christmas bells are ringing
And the little children are singing
For once again tis Christmas time
And the bells so sweetly chime
And out through the wild air
The music seems everywhere
The little children their stockings hang
Around the fireplace where they danced and sang
On that bright Christmas Eve
For they felt sure Santa would leave
Candy and toys for the girls and boys
To have fun and make some noise
On that bright Christmas Day

It Makes No Difference With Santa
By Julia B. Walker   1930

I know I'm very little
Folks say I shouldn't care
For it makes no difference with Santa
He visits everywhere
I know he leaves books and games
And toys for you and me
So don't you get frightened
Whether big or small
For I know Santa will visit us all.

Away In The Deepening Shadows

Julia B. Walker

Away in the deepening shadows
Away in the -----------------woods
Alone, alone with ----------------
In the midst -------------------stood

Seeking for something missing
Something gone from my soul
Something to give Jesus
My body as a whole

Once --------------------
At the age of nine
I entered a little country church
Where the grape vines twine

I gave my soul to Jesus
A life for Him, to live
Of bringing lost ones to the fold
And loving kindness give

I was baptized in the river
My sins were washed away
I promised I'd be true to Him
And never go astray

But now I've broken my promise
I've wandered from the fold
I've left the country church house
My soul to the devil sold

And now my mother has left me
My father's in his grave

Now I must look to Jesus
And try my soul to save

I cannot turn to Mother
And rest my head upon her knee
She's gone and left me on earth
My own faults to see

She used to tell me wished
That I would obey
The Lord and try to serve Him
In my work each day

But I would not listen
I turned from her side
Now I'm alone to see my faults
Since my mother died

I know my mother loves me
My father as well
So now you've heard my story
I was eager to tell

I've changed my ways, as Mother said
She wished that I would do
I'll always and forever
To my Savior be true

I have kept my promise
I've found comfort at last
He's taken me into the fold
And forgotten all my past

I am thankful, very thankful
To Mother and all

Just because I answered
To my Savior's call

And I hope that in the end
Mother's wish will come true
And I'll meet her in heaven
As she wanted me to do.

(----illegible)

Have You Noticed the Sun Shining Brightly?

Have you noticed the sun shining Brightly
Then a cloud comes and covers its face
It may continue for hours on end
Then it moves and the sun shines again

Compare it with life Brother Sister
Did His Son once shine Brightly thru you
But a cloud has obscured Him from sight
And your life seems as dark as the nite

Be up and doing my Brother
And clear all the dark clouds away
Repentance and courage and sunshine
And your life then will be as the day

All Things Work Together For Good

A soul whom Jesus pardoned
And washed away all sin
Looked up to Him in burning love
And bade Him to come in

Satan very much displeased
Did vow that he would cool
That burning love in the heart
And after a while he'd rule

Sin was hateful to this soul
And this old Satan knew
So planned to try another line
Carelessness would do.

He told him he's too busy
Didn't quite have time to pray
Had so very much to do
Fore the ending of the day.

Then when evening cometh
Weary with toils of the day
Sleep would overcome him
While on his knees to pray.

Still he read the Word of God
But his tho'ts oft went astray
Thinking of the chores ahead
Or the burdens of the day.

Soon praying was neglected
His Bible reading, too
The joy was not there as before
And love had leaked out, too.

But God in His great mercy
Looked down in tender love
And sent a trial so severe
From His own hand above

That he might be awakened
To the danger he was in
And he might seek His God for help
Fore he went back in sin.

The wind almost destroyed him
The flames tried to consume
The waters came near to overflow
Til it seemed he'd met his doom

Then stirred from his carelessness
Loudly on God did he call
Repenting and bitterly weeping
That he had neglected at all

Love once more burned in his heart
But with it too came shame
That he'd neglected his dear Lord
And reproached His name

Good had come from the trial
So Jesus stilled the storm
And as the light grew brighter
He glimpsed His precious form.

In everything now God is first
His praises he sings all day
There's a motto in this story
Where there's a will there's a way.

If you will to please the Saviour
He will always make a way
If you wont let Satan hinder
As you walk the pilgrim way.

Christ will be there with you always
And will never let you down
He will go with you to glory,
And present you with a crown.

(Poet's Note on later copy
  "This was written many years before it truly happened to
the author, Judy Tinsman").

At School

At school, we learn the golden rule
To read and write and spell
Arithmetic and English and
The sciences as well

And then we sing the hymns of praise
And read the Holy Word
But the most important is
That we obey the Lord

What we do, we know He sees us
What we say, we know He hears us
Where we go, what we think, how we act, He knows
So in our work or in our play
Our teacher gives a nod
Don't forget we're practicing
The presence of our God.

Teacher, Teacher

Teacher, Teacher come here quick
Mary fell down on a stick
Johnny poked Bill in the eye
Jerry make Leona cry

And I need help with my shoe
Betty Mae needs your help too
Jimmy cannot find his hat
Someone stole my ball and bat

Steven's chewing chewing gum
Jeffrey bro't to school his gun
Helen cheated while at play
These things make up the teachers day

But we're glad that we can call
On our teacher, after all
She's just mama in disguise
Wonder how she got so wise

There Is Beauty In A Rose
1954

There is beauty in a rose
That sends fragrance in the air
And by smelling of that fragrance
We know the rose is there.

There is beauty in a Christian
Whose life is like a perfume rare
By the sweetness and the goodness
We know that Christ is there

                        Mother,
                        Judy Tinsman

(Poet's Note on page
"Written February 8, 1954
for Jo Ann's autograph book").

If Flowers Know How To Bloom So Bright
1962

If flowers know how to bloom so bright
And birds know how to sing Thy praise
Then, surely, Lord You can show me how
    To serve You all my days.

God knows how to give blessings
And who to give them to
And He gave just such a blessing
    When He gave your parents - you.

(Poet's Note on page
Judy Tinsman
"February 23, 1962
Written for Vinnie Covington's autograph book)

Has God Done Nothing For You?

Has God done nothing for you
Could it be His Word is not true
He says He'll keep you each day
And guide you all the way
Has God done nothing for you?

Let others know then.

Look Up

May I keep my eyes on Jesus
Never lower let them be
Lest I see things round about
That would only hinder me

May I never try to carry
More than Christ would have me to
Lest the burden be too heavy
And His will I could not do

Someday

Someday, perhaps we'll understand
Why God has let us suffer so
With broken hearts we cry aloud
"Why, Lord, Oh why, I do not know"

"Deliver me," we pray to Him
And try to trust as best we can
And when we do not then receive
We cry, "I do not understand"

Perhaps we do not trust enough
And in our hearts do not believe
The miracle is already done
It's as we trust that we receive

So strengthen us as on we go
And help us Lord our load to bear
Help us completely trust in Thee
Until we see Thy face so fair.

(Poet's Note on page
"Written just before Jerry was born
June 1945")

This Day Brings Back Old Memories

This day brings back old memories
Of a few years back
Not yet a score
When one used to come to our house
But he don't come anymore.

We did so enjoy his coming
We felt enriched,
The love did flow
But he's been gone 3 years or more
And, oh, we miss him so.

His smile was oh, so kindly
His eyes did twinkle
His voice was low
He was our example and counsel
Oh, why did you have to go

Perhaps it was us who l----- him
His love not real,
His trust not true,
But, oh, how much we miss him
Wish he'd come and be as he used to do

We'd like to turn back time's hands
But time changes
All things they say
But our hearts are yearning and longing
For the good times of yesterday.

(--- *illegible*)

God Careth For His Own

We may boast and say we're sure
    Our faith will take us through
But we're only as strong as we prove to be
    In the tests that we go through

A chain is only just as strong
    As its weakest link, we know
So the tests and trials of life must come
    That the weak might stronger grow.

Tho' the night be long and winds are high
    And billows leap and foam
Be not dismayed, 'twill soon be day
    God careth for His own.

(Poet's Note on page
"February, 1952
After Johnny and Hubert were so sick with the flu")

My Only Hope Is Jesus
January 25, 1953

My only hope is Jesus
There's no other in this land
That I can trust to lean on
Or trust His guiding hands

My only hope is Jesus
No other voice so dear
I've set my ear to listen
No other voice to hear

I need Thy help dear Jesus
To keep me in the way
I know not where I'm going
Unless Thou lead the way

My only hope is Jesus
Without Him I am lost
Too many follow others
At such an awful cost

I do not ask for honor
Or praise of any man
I only ask dear Jesus
Thou would lead me by the hand

If there is some small corner
That Thou would have me fill
Where I could work unnoticed
And do Thy holy will

Then point me to that corner
Not with glory nor with fame

But just to follow Jesus
And glorify His name.

Tho' I suffer, Blessed Jesus

Tho' I suffer, blessed Jesus
Thou has suffered, too, for me
And if by my suffering, Father
I bring glory unto Thee

Teach me then, O Lord, to suffer
Give me Victory every day
If my suffering draws me closer
Closer then to Thee I'll stay

True sometimes my steps may falter
Tho' determined I may be
Jesus knows my every weakness
All my care I cast on Thee

I may weary with the trial
Feel I cannot bear the pain
Yet, I know when suffering's over
I'll see sunshine through the rain.

Soon Time Will Be Over

Soon time will be over
And your chance will be gone
Your life here be ended
And time to go home
But where will that be
And O' where will you go
Too late, then, too late
You'd regret you said no.

We Are Headed For The Judgment

The sun shall be darkened
And the moon not give her light
The stars will fall from heaven
Right in our very sight
So be careful my dear people
You will sure reap what you've sowed
We are headed for the judgment
Just a short way down the road

The sea and waves are roaring
Men's hearts failing them for fear
The powers of heaven shaken
And perilous times are here
The end is surely coming
When you'll reap as you've sowed
We are headed for judgment
Just a short way down the road

Are you ready for the judgment?
Are you in the narrow way?
Do you live your life for Jesus?
As you travel day by day.
Just remember you'll be judged
By the seeds that you have sowed
We are heading for the judgment
Just a short way down the road.

As You Look About You
September, 1967

As you look about you
Finding fault with one or two
Consider what would the church be like
If all were just like you.

Would there be more giving
More prayer on bended knee
More self denial and more love
If all were just like me

I think life would be more simple
More encouragement we'd find
If instead of faulting others
We'd look on what is "mine".

Is "mine" true humility
Is "mine" a heart of love
Is "mine" the very Spirit of Christ
Come down from above

What do other people think
When they look on me
The bride of Christ in shining white
Or is it only me

Is it the "I" that speaks so loud
That Christ they cannot see
My Friend, what would the church be like
If all were just like me

Many Things I Do Not Know Nor Understand
December 25, 1988

Many things I do not know nor understand
What will come tomorrow as I hold His hand
But this I know that He will never, never leave me
Why He loves me so I'll never understand

I was wretched, a worthless sinner and so blind
Jesus came and spoke to me and was so kind
Why He called me, why He loved me, when I was nothing
Such love as this, in others I will never find

I am glad, I can say, I still can feast
On His Word, and grow thereby, tho' I'm the least
Tests may come, and trials hard, and tribulation
He'll take me thru, for I'm His child, tho' yet the least

I felt His kiss, and I have never been the same
Tho' at the time I was poor, naked, blind and lame
My soul thrilled and I reached up to Him forever
I want to live so I'll bring honor to His name

Too Late

Gathered round her casket
Shedding many a tear
Speaking words of kindness
She wanted so much to hear

Neglected while she's living
Oft breathed their name in prayer
No flowers while she's living
Now flowers everywhere

Oft tears wet her pillow
Lonely, heartbroken, in bed
They didn't come to see her
Until after she was dead

She didn't know you loved her
Or that you really care
Only the friends and neighbors
          See flowers everywhere.

To Hub
(From Judy)
September 7, 1993

Today is your birthday
But, Honey, you are gone
You're at home with Jesus
And I am here alone

Oh! How much I miss you
As each day passes by
I touch the things that were yours
And then I weep and cry

Relatives have been kind to me
Friends and neighbors, too
But without our children
I don't know what I'd do

I remember little things you did
And things you used to say
And I have precious memories
As I think of you today

Good times we had together
There were hard times, too
But we worked together
And managed to pull through

You worked so hard, Daddy,
To provide for your own
And we were all - Oh, so glad
When Daddy was at home

God has been good to us
And we're truly not alone
Daddy's up there waiting
For His family to come home

So, rest my precious darling
You aren't now in pain
And someday in the great beyond
I hope to meet again

Your lonely wife
Judy Tinsman
Written on your birthday, September 7, 1993

My Darling Hub
September 7, 1995

In tears I saw you sinking
And watched you fade away.
My heart was nearly broken
I wanted you to stay.
God looked around His garden,
And found an empty place.
Then looked down upon this earth,
And He saw your tired face.
He put His arms around you
And lifted you to rest,
God's garden must be beautiful,
He only takes the best.
He knew how you were suffering,
And how much you were in pain
And knew that you would never
Get well on earth again.
Your resting place I visit.
And tend with loving care,
No on knows the heartache
When I turn and leave you there.
But someday, Dear, we'll meet again
On Heaven's Golden Shore
With outstretched arms you'll greet me there
With joy forever more.

　　　　　　　　Sadly missed by wife, Judy

(Poet's note on page
"September 7th, 1995
  Placed on Hub's tombstone)

Mother's   Musings

SONGS

What Can I Do
October 1985

I can't sing with the voice of an angel
I can't play the organ, harp, or viol
But I can give each a hearty handshake
And open my home with a smile.

I can't preach His precious Word with holy fervor
I can't explain the Scriptures like I'd like to do
But I can speak a loving word to a lost one
And show him One who'll always take him thro'

I can't lead, nor am I an organizer
I can't speak effectively to rouse a crowd
But I can pray and praise my Lord for His mercy
With tears, upon my knees, and my head bowed.

I can't give of my thousands, gold or silver
I can't give to worthy causes, house or land
But I can go into the home of a sick one
And cook and clean and give a helping hand

I can't go across the sea as missionary
I can't bury one who's lived his life and gone
But I can talk and pray with one who is discouraged
And help him to keep a holding on

I can't do many things as well as others
I can't do the job that God has given you
But I can testify to God's eternal goodness
I can do just what He asks me to do.
I can do just what He asks me to do.

Sweet Memories
Julia Walker

Once in early springtime
Strolling down a garden path
Seeing things that brought back
Memories of my boyhood
And that old sweetheart of mine
Memories of our rendez-vous
In the shadow of the pine

Chorus:
>   Sweetheart come back to me
>   And love me as before
>   Come to me with a promise
>   To leave me no more.

But that was years ago
When I was just a boy
When she was my sweetheart
My life, my love, my joy.
But she's rose to fame and fortune
And left me far behind
Forgotten all about me
Another love to find.

So now in this old world
I'll live my life alone
Treasuring dreams of the past
As pure as heaven above
This song tells its story
As many told before
Of a lover and his sweetheart
Parted from days of yore.

Tomorrow
June, 1995

Chorus:
Tomorrow, Tomorrow
May never be for me
I may go out to meet my deeds
Into eternity

I
If you have a duty, friends
Don't put it off too late
If you need to ask forgiveness
Do it now, please don't wait
If hasty words were spoken
And the hurt you caused went deep
Contact that one with humble heart
'Fore you lay you down to sleep

II
If you have been deceitful, friend
Not honest in every way
Maybe it was a little white lie
But you got things your way
Maybe you carried a tale that you
Didn't know was true
Whatever your problem is, my friend
Do now what you must do.

III
If you have never known the Lord
Or known His special care
If you're burdened down with sins
And there's no help anywhere
Then turn to Jesus standing by

He knows the way you go
He'll welcome you, forgive your sins
And make you white as snow

You're Gonna Reap Just What You Sow

1
In your conduct, in your dress
Or helping others in distress
It's important what you do and what you say
God knows the reason why
If you caused someone to cry
And you'll answer for it in that judgment day

Chorus   You're gonna reap, you're gonna reap
                    Gonna reap just what you sow.

2
Someone's watching where you go
Who it is you might not know
You're gonna reap, you're gonna reap just what you sow
If you lead someone astray
You're gonna answer in that day
You're gonna reap, you're gonna reap just what you sow.

3
If someone's lost because of you
Then, my friend, what will you do
You're gonna reap, you're gonna reap just what you sow
You're an example to someone here
And it could be someone dear
You're gonna reap, you're gonna reap just what you sow.

4
If there's a question, then say no
Just ask Jesus 'fore you go
Your decision might help someone on the way
Live the life the Word commands
Then you're in the Savior's hands
He will help you to be true 'til your last day.

Are You Humble

1
Do you think you're humble, and lowly as our Lord
Can you have peace and joy within, living to His word.

2
Can you be contented, when your sincere will
Is trampled down by others, are you rejoicing still.

3
Or do the tears begin to start, and does self-pity flow
When you tell your troubles, so other folks will know.

4
Would you pamper then your flesh, have others do so, too
Be hurt and feel neglected, when no one notices you.

5
You may suffer a little slight, and some your name revile
But if Humility dwells within, you still can wear a smile.

O' Come To The Saviour

O' come to the Saviour
Don't turn Him away
Don't grieve His spirit
By telling Him nay
Your heart's growing harder
With each passing day
O' won't you tell Him
You'll nevermore stray

Chorus
O' come to the Saviour
Why will you say no
Come to the Saviour
Before you go
O' let Him cleanse you
From sin and from woe
O' come to the Saviour
Please don't say no

O' come to the Saviour
True friend He will be
O' He has promised
To not forsake thee
His promise is true
Cause He's proved it to me
O' come to the Saviour
No regrets will there be

God surely is calling
And oft is the time
He talked to your heat
Through song and thro' rhyme
In sermons and prayers

God is pleading with you
In shame drop your head
For you know it is true

Why shake your head no
When He's longing for you
And O' we are pleading
We want you saved, too
Please won't you consider
Just now, 'fore you go
While Jesus is calling
Please don't tell Him no.

If You Miss Heaven You'll Miss It All

If you're tired of sinning'
Take your Savior's hand
There's a mansion worth winnin'
In a great promised Land
Many doubters are grinnin'
Don't you slip and fall
If you miss heaven
You'll miss it all

Chorus
If you miss heaven you'll miss it all
For me to reach heaven I'll gladly crawl
The smallest and weakest who love Him are tall
If you miss heaven you'll miss it all.

Our loving Savior gave earth a second birth
And His salvation frees us from the sorrows of earth
Forever with Jesus make clouds seem so small
If you miss heaven you'll miss it all

Chorus

Closer to Jesus

1
The Saviour is dearer to me every day
The closer I live to Him
And brighter His glory illumines my way
The closer I live to Him.

Chorus
Closer to Him, Closer to Him
I want to live closer to Jesus
There's no one so precious, so faithful to me
And I want to live closer to Him.

2
His service grows sweeter and sweeter to me
The closer I live to Him
And more of His goodness and mercy I see
The closer I live to Him.

3
I long more and more in His likeness to be
The closer I live to him
And sure that I am, that His face I shall see
The closer I live to Him.

All My Life For Him

Close your eyes and go to sleep my baby
While Grandma sings to you a lullaby
While you're resting on my shoulder I will tell you
Things in my life that has goneby

I was born poor in a large family
And I grew up as timid as can be
I always wished that I could rise above that load
Be accepted, be clean and filled with purity

When nine years old, we went to a revival
At the altar call, I was kneeling there
God spoke peace to this tender heart in girlhood
And I never meant to stray away from there

My family was not a Christian family
I had no one to guide me in the life
So, in time I lost the joy of my salvation
And went into the world of ---- and strife.

But God's spirit never ever really left me
And often pleaded with me when I was alone
But my heart had turned to fashion and folly
And my heart had somewhat harder grown.

Then my Father in His tender loving mercy
Sent heartache grief and sorrow o'er and o'er
'Till I looked around for someone who could help me
And then is when I found The Lord, the open door.

Many years have passed since that blessed moment
Many blessings I've received from His dear hand

And I've never once regretted that I yielded
And joined the little group, the Christian Band.

As I look back and start reminiscing
And see how God has been so good to me
With deep regret I recall all my failures
But my Advocate has borne them all for me.

So, to one and all I recommend my Saviour
You'll not find a better friend in all this earth
It's been years now since I first knew Him
And became partaker of the 2nd birth

And every day He proves that He loves me
Every moment, every breath I'll spend for Him
And be found doing just the work He gave me
When my steps are feeble and my eyes are dim.

Whether death calls or I remain to see Him
When He comes shouting and descending in the air
I must be ready to rise up and meet Him
And, so be forever with Him there.

(---- *illegible*)

Are You Really His
- An earlier draft of this song is entitled
"Questions"

1
There's some questions I would like to ask you
The answers you can know in your heart
But think and consider each question
For the Lord knows each one apart.

Chorus
Do you really own His name
Or is it just the one you claim
For its blessings that might come to you.
Are you really now His own
Flesh of flesh and bone of bone
Does your life belong to Him or you

2
Does the Lord have first place in your affections
In your plans for the night and the day
In your buying and selling and speaking
Is the Lord consulted alway

3
Do you ask Him each day for His guidance
And then go and do as you please
Are you burdened for sinners and praying
For the blood that cleanses and frees

4
If Jesus would ask you to suffer
That glory might be brought to His name
That a little lost sheep be delivered
Would you bear the cross and the shame

2nd   Chorus - after last stanza
Are you really now His own
Or is your heart as hard as stone
Claiming what long ago slipped away
A profession will not do
Jesus will not be with you
Cast yourself at His feet, be saved today.

I Walked Alone

I walked alone with tears and sorrows
I walked alone my heart did break
Until I learned there was A Saviour
Who died on Calvary for my sake

Chorus
    O praise the Lord, O, Glory, glory
For all my Lord has done for me
    Forgave my sins and cleansed me Holy
Broke my bonds and set me free

I walked in sin, no satisfaction
No peace, contentment, did I find
I searched in vain for earthly pleasure
To satisfy A longing soul.

At School

At school, we learn the golden rule
To read and write and spell
Arithmetic and English and
The sciences as well

And then we sing the hymns of praise
And read the Holy Word
But the most important is
That we obey the Lord

What we do, we know He sees us
What we say, we know He hears us
Where we go, what we think,
How we act, He knows

So in our work or in our play
Our teacher gives a nod
Don't forget we're practicing
The presence of our God.

(Poet's Notes on later copy
"Written by Judy Tinsman
For last day of school
program").

Chorus: Talked in 3 parts
What we do (part1) we know (part2) He sees us (part3)
What we say (part2) we know (part1) He hears us (part3)
Where we go (part1) what we think (part2)
How we act (part3) He knows (ALL)

Watering Flowers In The Garden Of Love

1.   Watering flowers in the garden of love
Watering flowers for the Saviour above
Watering flowers by the tears that we shed,
The flowers are His who suffered and bled

2.   Can we do less as we journey below,
Than help someone else, as onward we go
You know our tears, our work and our prayers
Will meet us up there, on the golden stairs

3.   Then brother get down and cry out to God
To prepare you to walk where the saints have trod
Get down at the cross, low down at his feet
Then the tears that we shed will be exceedingly sweet

4.   Perhaps there is one who is watching your life
A brother, or child, sister, husband or wife
It even may be a stranger to you,
Who is watching so close everything that you do.

5.   If things go wrong in your pathway of life
If others cause you trouble and strife,
If your plans fail, friends turn from your face,
Then look up to God, and ask for more grace.

6.   If affliction should come, or sickness or death,
Or poverty knocks to destroy all our faith,
Then the tears and the work for others you do
By the mercies of God will be sent to unto you.

7.   Watering flowers may seem hard to you,
But our Father knows what's good for you

Then do your best, what He asks you to do,
For as you give, shall be given to you.

YOU NEED JESUS TODAY
May 1, 1965

1   When trouble or heartache oppress you,
Will Jesus be close by your side
To comfort and strengthen you onward,
Or have you cast Him aside?
'Til Jesus has gone on before you
And now He is far up the way
Your time you have wasted on pleasure
Oh, how you need Jesus today.

2   Mother holds her sick baby
With pain and a feverish brow
In distress she cries unto Jesus
She's willing for help from Him now
And someday you'll know you need Jesus
When He whispers now won't you come
The troubles are many in a lifetime
Trust Him and He'll guide you home

3   A man gave his heart unto Jesus
Then later drifted away
His son overseas in the army
Is needing his dad's prayers today
His dad's heart has grown cold and formal
His prayers never reaching the skies
Without hope, without help, without Jesus
His son on the battlefield dies

4   A young couple in love with each other
Never taking the Lord in account
He would lead them and make their life happy
By His blood in the soul cleansing fount
But they have no time now for Jesus

Other things more important to do
But some day when you need Him sorely
He may have not time for you.

5.   Young people are you looking to Jesus
To choose your career in this life
Whether He would have you remain single,
Or choose you a husband or wife?
Oh children the Lord dearly loves you
Won't you yield to the Saviour today,
In His presence no harm can come near you
For Jesus will stand in the way.

6   The years have gone by as I see him
This old man so aged and bent
All his years he'd thought of salvation
To accept it before life was spent
But satan has kept him so busy
With the pleasures and cares of this life,
'Til in death satan shouts in glee to him
You've lost the pearl of great price.

7   Her hands are all wrinkled and care worn
She's mothered a large family
In her youth she learned to love Jesus
And taught each of her babies to pray
But as time went by she was careless
In prayer and in trusting in God
Now her children are praying for mother
To be saved 'fore she's laid 'neath the sod.

8   Many pictures of life could be painted
Of failure because we forget God
But we hope these few will suffice you
'Fore you fall 'neath the chastening rod

Whether old or young doesn't matter
There's a time set apart for each one
When Jesus in love gently beckons
Don't wait 'til your time is gone

9   If you never knew Jesus accept Him
While He's calling upon you today
You may need Him in a moment of trouble
And you may not have time to pray
If once you've known Him in your lifetime
But was careless or drifted away
Come back while there's life and hope for you
Lest time soon be ended for aye

        Repeat
When trouble or heartache oppress you
Will Jesus be close by your side
To comfort and strengthen you onward
Or have you cast Him aside
'Til Jesus has gone on before you
And now He is far up the way
Your time you have wasted on pleasure
Oh, you need Jesus today

Addition to above song May 2, 1965 Sun. nite

10   There is one and we thank God for her
When we see her grey head bowed in prayer
Praying while others are sleeping
Earnest prayer and tears mingle there
She has a son out there yonder
Living in the pleasures of sin
She's pleading and willilng to suffer
To see her boy brought unto Him

11 Her heart is so pure and so holy
The temptations of sin can't annoy
She's pleading and praying to Jesus
"God save my wondering boy"
You don't like to think of tomorrow
Or to think of that great judgment day
That's why we're trying to warn you
'Fore time has vanished away.

I Sing Because I'm Happy

Two hands to do God's bidding
Two feet to take me to
Wherever He would have me go
To the work He'd have me do.

Two eyes to see God's handiwork
Two lips to tell it, too
Two ears to hear God's gentle voice
As He shows me how to do

All I own I'm wealthy
That's why today I sing,
I'm happy and protected 'cause
I'm a child now of the King

Testimony Time

Has God done nothing for you
Could it be His Word is not true
He says He'll keep you each day
And guide you all the way
Has God done nothing for you?

Let others know then.

Fighting In The Army Of The Lord.
So you think

I'm fighting in the army of the Lord
I keep the doctrine strait by His Word
    If my brothers cannot see
    And with me they don't agree
Then I'm <u>fighting</u> in the army of the Lord.

I'm fighting in the army of the Lord
With much earnestness I'll wield the sword
    I'll not greet him with a kiss
    And his presence I'll dismiss
'<u>Cause</u> I'm fighting in the army of the Lord.

I'm fighting in the army of the Lord
I'll break the love that binds us as a cord
    If they will not come my way
    Then they just can go astray
For I'm <u>fighting</u> in the army of the Lord.

I'm fighting in the army of the Lord
My fellowship for them I can't afford
    When I preach to them the don't
    And come my way they wont
Well, I'm <u>fighting</u> in the army of the Lord.

You're fighting in the army of the Lord?
By preaching letter and not the spirit of the Word
    Your brother shows a spirit sweet
    Yet your brother you'll not greet
Are you fighting in the army of the Lord?

So you're fighting in the army of the Lord
You cry aloud and spare not the sword

You wound and do not bind
The lost you do not find
Are you fighting in the army of the Lord.

You're fighting in the army of the Lord
By example of our dear and precious Lord
    Do you reject whom He rejects
    And accept whom He accepts
While you're fighting in the army of the Lord.

You're fighting in the army of the Lord
Do your messages all come from the Word
    You will neither break nor bend
    And to Hell you'll surely send
Those not fighting in <u>your</u> army of the Lord.

You're fighting in the army of the Lord
O' Consider your spirit by His Word
    If a brother you would win
    Give your heart and life for Him
Then you're fighting in the army of the Lord.

You're fighting in the army of the Lord
We want no compromising of the Word
    We want to know that you care
    About His people everywhere
Then we'll join you in the army of the Lord.

Quicksand And Sin

1.   This world and it follies
It calls out a dare
Come and taste and enjoy
But it is like quicksand
'Twill swallow you up
Ah, God save that girl or boy.

2.   The sand looks so harmless
There by the seashore
But it is deadly for you
So the world and its pleasure
Inch by inch you are gone
Where there is no help for you.

3.   O, send out the warning
To all who will hear
There is danger that way
We don't want you caught
In the devil's sandtrap
In eternity you will say

Chorus
O, Won't someone pray
They're sinking today
And soon will be out of sight
O, won't someone pray
When he first sees them stray
Lest they be lost in the nite.

Why?

Chorus
Why Jesus loves me
I do not know
But wherever I am I
Want Him to go

1
Why don't you love me
When I love you so
We're brothers and sisters
One family you know
Born of His Spirit
Washed in His blood
Our sins all forgiven
In the cleansing flood.

Why don't you accept me
Because I can't see
Every jot and tittle
As it seems to thee
Why can't you be patient
And pray for me.
Live a life so humble
You're convincing to me.

So long as our hearts
Are bound together
So long as we live
For Jesus Christ
God can take care of
Every difference
Whether doctrine, con-
Viction or bias.

In This Life There Are Disappointments

1
In this life there are disappointments
Our plans sometimes go astray
Our trust in our friends sometimes fail us
Have you failed Jesus today

Chorus
Is the disappointment in you?
Have you kept your heart always true
Have you stood the test
Have you done your best
Is the disappointment in you?

2
Now we all are God's little children
He has a plan for each one
Are we doing our best to fulfill it
By the time that your life here is done.

3
As a father makes plans for his children
And plans for them only the best
So God has a plan for His children
Of sweet peace and eternal rest.

4
To each He has given a duty
That nobody else can perform
If you turn your back on your life's plan
'Twould be better if he'd not been born.

Trust Always
August 20, 1962

If you can trust Him when the birds are singing,
If you can trust Him when the sun is shining bright,
If you can trust Him when your heart is full of gladness,
Can't you trust Him then when it is night?

Can't you trust Him when the storms are raging?
Can't you trust Him when all you friends have gone?
If you can't trust Him with troubles all about you
How can you trust Him when your life is done?

Can't you trust Him when your life is full of sorrow
When seems the aching heart will never cease to be?
Can't you trust Him with bereavement pangs upon you
If not, O' then what can He trust with thee?

Can you trust Him with afflictions sore upon you?
Can you trust Him when your loved ones turn you down?
Can you trust Him with your name cast out as evil?
No, then can He trust you with a starry crown?

If we'll trust the Lord in everything while living
In our joy, sorrow, grief and all the rest
If we'll trust Him without a doubt or murmur
'Twill be easy to trust Him in death.

"Old House"

Aged body in a casket
No one lives there any more
Life has left that aged body
Soul fled to the other shore

Oh, if you could only speak
Wondrous stories you could tell
Of little bits of heaven
Or a life that seemed as hell

You could tell of grief and heartache
You could tell of love and joy
You have surely witnessed death
Seen the birth of girl or boy

Oh, if you could speak to us
Of memories through the years
Would the laughter and the gladness
Outweigh the grief and tears

Lord, Take Me And Make Me What You'd Have Me To Be

Lord, take me and make me what you'd have me to be
I'm willing to be molded, Lord Jesus, by Thee
You can take from or add to what ever it takes
To be able to use me for your dear name's sake.

Chorus
I know that I'm yours, Lord
You've always been true
I'm grateful to know, Lord
That you'd see me thru'
So I'm asking, precious Jesus
You'll hear when I call
Hold fast to my hand, Lord
That I never will fall

I've been often defeated but I want to be true
To know that I'm pleasing, blessed Jesus to you
To be used in your kingdom and help it expand
To say, do or go, Lord, only at your command

That my tho'ts may be pleasing, my heart may be true
I might be a blessing and a pleasure to You
That I might help others, as I walk the last mile
And when I see Glory, I'll see Your sweet smile

Jesus Was There
1978

1
I've been thru the valley of weeping
I've been to the depths of despair
I've been where no human could help me
But I found Jesus there.

2
Many are the times since I found Him
I've encountered hard things to bear
But never since that blessed moment
Has Jesus failed to be there

3
When the cares of life pressed upon me
Sometimes I neglected to pray
And found myself in deep trouble
But Jesus was faithful alway

4
I know many times I have failed Him
Remorse often floods o'er my soul
But He says, "My child I forgive you"
And then again I am whole.

5
My name has been cast out as evil
Rejected by those that I love
Accused by the accuser of the brethren
But loved by the One up above

6

I mean to stay true and faithful
Each day I ask for more grace
When I pass from Time to Eternity
I'll see Him face to face.

The Steps That I Must Retrace

1
On the hill Difficulty
Christian went to sleep
When he got to the top
He started to weep
He'd lost his soul
Prayed for forgiveness and grace
To learn a good lesson
From the steps he had to retrace

2
Now Christian and Hopeful
They walked in the way
When the going was rough
They took a by way
In Doubting Castle
Prayed for forgiveness and grace
And deliverance from doubts
By the steps they had to retrace

3
O, Brother, take courage
If you've gone to sleep
Or stepped out of the way
When the going was steep
If you'll repent
And pray for forgiveness and grace
You'll learn precious lessons
From the steps you have to retrace

Chorus
O the steps you have to retrace
God will give you courage and grace

Precious are the lessons I'm learning
From the steps I've had to retrace

4
If you've been overtaken
And the battle you lost
Don't give up the struggle
Consider the cost
You need God's help
Pray for forgiveness and grace,
The way'll be more precious
By the steps you have to retrace

Where Can One Find The Saviour?
Where, Oh, Where Is Jesus?

1
Where can one find the Saviour
In this old world down here?
Oh, where is He hiding
The One they say is dear?

2
I've been down to the movies
And didn't find Him there
I went to the carnival
But He did not come near

3
I went to the swimming pool
No trace of Him did find
Where, Oh, where is Jesus
That I can make Him mine?

4
They said He could be found at church
In the pulpit up so high
So I sought out the largest one
But it almost made me cry

5
Instead was pride and fashion
A self-righteous attitude
But no where was the Saviour
And no soul building food

6
So I left with tears and longing
Walked the river side
Still looking for a Saviour
To come in and abide

7
There were pleasure cruises
And close by a county fair
Nudity and gambling
But no Jesus there

8
So I turned and walked away
And in my mind could see
All things this world call pleasure
No salvation there for me

9
I could see the painted faces
I could see the cigarette
I could see the dance, the mug of beer
But no salvation yet

10
So I walked from all I saw
No contentment there
Still looking for a Saviour
But now, where, oh, where?

11
I went into my closet
And shutting then the door
I fell sobbing on my knees
To seek the world no more

12
And there I found Jesus
And there He spoke to me
If ye love the world
Then ye cannot love me

13
Oh yes, I found my Saviour
And He's so dear to me
From this world and all its pleasures
My Christ has set me free

Chorus
Where, Oh, where is Jesus?
With Him I would not part
I find that in a righteous man
Christ dwells in His heart

Old House

1

Old house with broken windows
Hinges broken on the door
'Tis deserted, falling down
No one lives there anymore

2

Oh, if you could only speak
Wondrous stories you could tell
Of little bits of heaven
Or life that seemed as hell.

3

You could tell of grief and heartache
You could tell of love and joy
You have surely witnessed death
Seen the birth of girl and boy

4

Families grown from childhood
Have scattered far and wide
Some to fame and fortune
Some in disgrace abide

5

Some may have lived here
Acquainted with the Lord
Who knew the worth of prayer
And abode in His Word

6

Old house you may have had
Families that were worse

Who never heard the name of God
Except spoken in a curse

7
Old house if you could speak
Of memories through the years
Would the laughter, joy and gladness
Outweigh the grief and tears?

Love Each Other
October 8, 1989

1
I'm not always on the mountaintop
I'm not shouting all the time
But I know that I belong to Him
And I know that He is mine

2
I'm not boasting in my righteousness
Nor do I say what I would do
But I love my precious Jesus
And to Him I would be true

3
In this life there will be problems
And I've come thru quite a few
In some of them I've stumbled
But in Him my hope renew

4
He has never, never left me
Nor forsaken now am I
So, I keep my eyes on heaven
And my goal is in the sky.

5
There are those who now despise me
And they think my soul is lost
I'm not wanted in their company
By them I've been cast off.

6
And it hurts because I love them
And they are my very own
And I wish the very best for them
Pray, don't leave them all alone

7
I pray, Lord, you will guide them
In the strait and narrow way
Teach them the things they need to know
And help them not to stray

8
And as they walk the way of life
Open their eyes that they might see
And fill their hearts so with Your love
They'll look with love on me.

I'm The Least One
December, 1980

1
Tho' I'm the least one, yet, I know, Lord, I love You
Your slightest wish I want to fulfill
But I know many times I have grieved You
Make me perfect as I climb the last hill.

2
I know I'm worthless, yet, I know, Lord, You love me
May others know that I love you, too
And my heart longs to serve you much better
Let me know what You want me to do.

3
Tho' I'm nothing, yet, I know, Lord, you gave me
A tender spirit, a love so divine
And I hunger and thirst for more knowledge
Of Thy Word, Thy Way, all that's Thine.

Trust Instead Of Tears
August 18, 1962

In the pathway of life
There is trouble and strife
An thorns thickly sprinkle the way
But if we'll only look ahead
And see by whom we're led
Then all darkness will turn into day

Chorus
So Instead of our tears
Or pour our woes in others' ears
Let us go to our Jesus alone
He is able to do
All we need and more too
Let us ask all we need to be done

There is help for you there
When there's no help anywhere
He's ever listening each day for your cry
He'll never leave nor forsake
Nor the blessing from you take
'Til you leave for your home upon high

Don't be discouraged or blue
But just trust and be true
And life will be sweeter down here
When your time has come to go
Then your heart with love will flow
You'll be certain there's no need to fear

I Feel That As I Stand Here Singing

I feel that as I stand here singing
I want to see you saved too
My heart reaches out in love to you
That's why we try to warn you

You don't like to think of tomorrow
But enjoy the pleasures today
That's why we're praying and pleading
'Fore time has vanished away

Too Much Talk

1
Oh, be careful what you're saying
Falling now on children's ears
It will surely bring a harvest
Of future sorrow and bitter tears

2
So, you see something in your brother
And you sister does not so
And you talk in children's presence
The seed of gossip you now sow

3
You call it righteous indignation
So your tongue goes wagging on
And you talk in front of children
'Til all confidence is gone

4
Oh, my brother, Oh, my sister
Can you see what you have done?
In the minds of little children
Seeds of doubt now you have sown

5
So you pray and teach your children
This is right and this is wrong
Feeling all the time so righteous
While you sing your slander song

6
Don't you realize, my dear ones
You are what you think about?

While you talk of their shortcomings
Can you have the victory shout?

7
Oh, deceive us not, we're pleading
And we chatter, chatter on
On the faults and sins of others
Until the love of God is gone

8
God has shown us what to think on
Things that's lovely and are true
Of good report, praise and virtue
Are these the tho'ts that come to you?

9
And the one of whom you're speaking
Are the helped as you talk on?
Tattling all of this to others
Can they feel your love so warm?

10
Do you feel love warm and flowing
For the lost and those who fail
Or does your talking make you haughty
Your tongue become a whip and flail?

11
If on bended knee you're pleading
For that one that troubles you
Pray half as much as you once tattled
Then your love will be true

12
Now, deny yourself the pleasure
Of the wagging tattling tongue
But on your knees in fervent prayer
Stay, 'til the thing is done.

(Poet's Note on page
"Written during the terrible
conflict when the Devil was
dividing God's people).

Clouds Of Life

Have you noticed the sun shining brightly
Then a cloud comes and covers its face
It may continue for hours on end
Then it moves and the sun shines again

Compare it with life brother, sister
Did His Son once shine brightly thru you
But a cloud has obscured Him from sight
And your life seems as dark as the night

Chorus
Be up and doing my Brother
And clear all the dark clouds away
Repentance and courage and sonshine
And your life then will be as the day

(Poet's Note on later copy inserted "Chorus" and made
minor changes to the earlier poem - Have You Noticed The
Sun Shining Brightly).

As The Oldest Girl In The Family

Verse I
As the oldest girl in the family
Duties often were given to me
Such as care of the small ones and babies
While Mother was gone or busy
I did my best with these duties
Tho' mistakes I often have made
But for Father some would have been tragic
These memories sweet never fade

Such as the time I was trying to satisfy my baby sister,
Mary, who was cross, by carrying her around in the house
while the family was eating supper.   I was a thin little girl
and my arms became tired as I carried her, so I sat her
down on the library table to rest my arms a bit.   Her little
baby arms reached for the kerosene lamp and before I
could catch it, she knocked off the lamp chimney.   In a
moment the window curtains were blazing and then the
freshly papered ceiling, too.   I grabbed up my baby sister
and screamed.   Our father ran to the rescue.   Quickly he
grabbed a heavy comforter from the bed an smothered the
flames.   The danger was past.   The damage had been
done, true, but not beyond repair.   It could be restored.

Verse II
Now Mother has gone home to Glory
But duties I still have to do
Praying for brothers and sisters
To bring them home, Mother, to you.
Oh, Father, help me with the burden
Tho' mistakes I often have made
Oh, Father come to the rescue.
That these loved ones will be saved.

Open your ears to my crying
Open your heart to this plea
Give your heart to Jesus
And go home with Mother and me.

Children often will get into danger
The older ones must watch after them
So please don't think that I'm bossy
When I try to lead you from sin.
I'm only doing what Mother would have me
The Holy Father directs me the same
And beckon the angels in heaven
Come praise His holy name.

If I can't lead you to heaven
Then tell me who is to blame.

Farewell
January 31, 1978

Now the time has come for parting
And I don't know what to say
I've sung my songs and poems
On this tape for you today

Now, I know they're nothing extra
But just something that I had
Been writing these since girlhood
When I was happy or sad

And I tho't if I would sing them
And recite the poems, too
You could better understand me
And know what I've been thru

I've always wanted Jesus
Since just a little girl
I never wanted wealth or fame
Or things of this old world

I've done a lot of Bungling
Many mistakes I have made
But "I forgive you", says my Saviour
When my sin on Him was laid

So, I'll end this little discourse
As I send to you my love
Praying always to my Father
That we'll all meet above

(cont/)

We'll sing and shout and praise His name
Around Our Father's throne
And in that land of far off day
We'll know as we are known.